Presence in Chaos

365 Mindful Moments

Debra Sabatini Hennelly

Resiliti LLC
New Jersey USA

Debra Sabatini Hennelly

Presence in Chaos — 365 Mindful Moments by Debra Sabatini
Hennelly,
2nd edition, March 2020.
ISBN: 978-1-7345580-1-2 (paperback)

For my Parents

Frank and Sandra Sabatini, who taught me—and continue to show me—the value of keeping a sense of humor and positivity in the midst of challenges (or chaos); and of being present for those we love and those we serve, because time is a very precious gift.

Table of Contents

Introduction

As my 60th birthday rapidly approaches, I have become keenly aware of the passage of time. Sometimes, it feels like life has been a blur since my 20s—working hard, taking on challenging professional roles, getting married, starting a family, making a home, juggling commitments, and basically running as fast as I could on a treadmill that I didn't think I could stop for the last 30 years. A middle-aged over-achiever, lacking the perspective to know when to say, "enough already."

Each decade brought more opportunities to keep racing forward, taking on more responsibilities, going for the next rung on the ladder the next brass ring, keeping up with expectations, while also juggling all of the commitments that came with raising our three fabulous daughters. Mostly, life was a busy buzz from week to week, month to month, business goal to business goal, holiday to holiday, and birthday party to birthday party. Sometimes chaotic, sometimes just plain exhausting. Some of it was self-imposed; some of it came with the territory of working in law firms and corporate-land, surrounded by high-achievers and soccer-moms.

Trying to be everything to everyone seems to be an affliction that is not unique to women of a certain age; but, upon reflection, I can see that it's been one of my greatest weaknesses. There's that old cliché: "If you want something done, give it to a busy person." That was me. And I knew plenty of others who were just like me—and still do.

I have always been someone who looks forward, makes plans and works toward delivering on expectations—sometimes taking on more than I could accomplish without pulling all-nighters. Over the years, the tempo of my daily life took on the drumbeat of expert-level multi-tasking, while drinking from a fire hose of challenges as a corporate "change-agent." The background noise of 21st-century information-overload only heightened the stress of focusing on the essential. Staying ahead of commitments required doubling-down on work, racking up long hours and deferring on the things that renewed and energized me—family time, unplugging, rejuvenating, caring for my own well-being.

I needed a major reset to overcome the physical and mental drain of serious burnout—the kind that knocked me down for days, a week or longer. The universe had been sending me very loud signals for a while, and my survival instinct finally kicked in. "Put on your own oxygen mask before assisting the person next to you," right? I couldn't be effective at doing anything for anyone until I took the time to recharge my positivity and rebuild my resilience.

I needed to regroup. Get centered. And that's how this book was born.

Over the years, I had done a lot of reading in the self-help, personal development, and positive psychology fields. (Happy to share recommendations.) I pulled out those books and reminded myself of the rejuvenating powers of mindfulness and creativity. I committed to spending the first 30 minutes of every morning finding ways to just be "in the moment." Present. No email, no news, just quiet reflection. Focusing on my breath, being aware of my senses, but trying to be a detached "observer." Sometimes with soft music, sometimes just in silence. But I was hopelessly bad at quieting the running to-do list in my mind. So, I opted for a "Plan B" approach to rejuvenation: getting creative.

I've spent my professional life being a problem-solver, analyzing details, creating risk management systems; first as an engineer and then as a lawyer. Yet, I'm left-handed and right-brained (sounds like a professional mismatch, right?); and I have always loved being creative as a way of unplugging. I pulled out my paints and colored pencils, went through my years of photography projects—flowers, birds, sunrises, sunsets, places to which I've traveled. And I started writing again, too. I also started reading things for fun—not just for my work—and collecting quotes, poems and essays that inspire me. Focusing this way gave me a path to escape into the moment, away from the chaos around or ahead of me, without going anywhere.

At some point, 30 minutes became an hour or more. Now, it's become a sort of self-imposed therapy session first thing each morning, with my version of mindfulness that grounds me and helps me get my head on straight before taking on the day ahead. It's amazing how much more bandwidth this gives me for dealing with the surprises that can come with even the best-laid plans—and how much more productive I can be, even without multi-tasking.

A few years ago, I decided to start sharing with friends some of the inspirations and wisdom I'd read—just one thought each day. It was sort of like making my mindfulness commitment out loud to keep the discipline of it. Rather than just sharing quotations as plain text, though, I decided to use my own photography as a background to reflect something in each quote. After a while, I found the courage to share them publicly on social media; and, to my delightful surprise, I received some comments and even some shares. At this point, I'm into my third year of sharing these daily posts. A few times, when I'd let most of a day go by without sharing my post, I would get messages asking where it was; people were actually looking forward to what I was posting—what an amazing feeling!

I had been getting suggestions to collect my posts into a book, so here they are: a year's-worth of those I consider to be my better ones. I hope you enjoy them and that they inspire you to start your own mindful "moment"—whatever helps you to be quiet with yourself, get centered and energized to face the day ahead.

Be present with yourself, those you love and those you serve. Time is a finite resource, so it's a very precious gift.

AND NOW
LET US WELCOME
THE NEW YEAR,
FULL OF THINGS
THAT HAVE YET TO COME.
- RAINER MARIA RILKE

THE BEST WAY
TO PREDICT
THE FUTURE
IS TO INVENT IT.
-ALAN KAY

Great things are not done
by impulse,
but by a series of
small things
brought together.
- George Eliot

@debsabhen

LIFE IS LIKE
RIDING A BICYCLE.
TO KEEP YOUR BALANCE,
YOU MUST KEEP MOVING.
- ALBERT EINSTEIN

@debsabhen

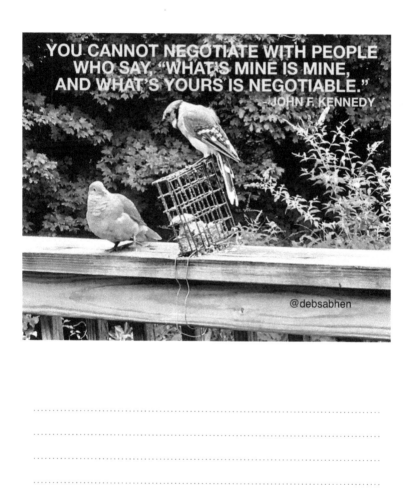

YOU CANNOT NEGOTIATE WITH PEOPLE
WHO SAY, "WHAT'S MINE IS MINE,
AND WHAT'S YOURS IS NEGOTIABLE."
-JOHN F. KENNEDY

@debsabhen

...YOU MAY HAVE A FRESH START ANY MOMENT YOU CHOOSE; FOR THIS THING THAT WE CALL "FAILURE" IS NOT THE FALLING DOWN, BUT THE STAYING DOWN.

— MARY PICKFORD

Jan 8

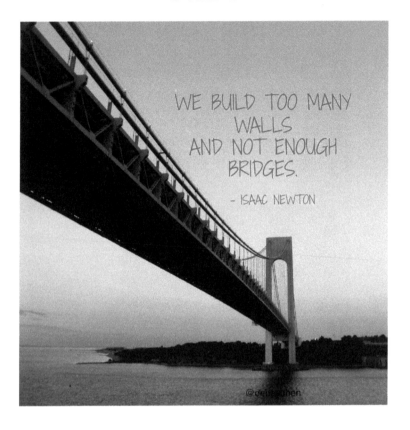

WE BUILD TOO MANY
WALLS
AND NOT ENOUGH
BRIDGES.

- ISAAC NEWTON

@detibauhen

The high road can be narrow and bumpy, but the view is magnificent.
- Dean Jackson

@debsablien

Imagine
if we treated each new dawn
of each new day
with the same reverence and joy
as we do each new year...
~ Angie Lynn

. . . .

. . . .

. . . .

. . . .

. . . .

. . . .

TO MAKE
A DIFFERENCE
IN SOMEONE'S LIFE,
YOU DON'T HAVE TO BE BRILLIANT,
RICH, BEAUTIFUL OR PERFECT.
YOU JUST HAVE TO CARE.

- MANDY HALE

@debsabhen

A YEAR FROM NOW,
YOU WILL WISH YOU HAD
STARTED TODAY.
– KAREN LAMB

@debsabhen

....
....
....
....
....
....

BE THANKFUL FOR PROBLEMS.
IF THEY WERE LESS DIFFICULT,
SOMEONE WITH LESS ABILITY
MIGHT HAVE YOUR JOB.
- JIM LOVELL

TRUST IS
LIKE THE AIR WE BREATHE.
WHEN IT'S PRESENT,
NO ONE REALLY NOTICES.
WHEN IT'S NOT THERE,
EVERYBODY NOTICES.
- WARREN BUFFETT

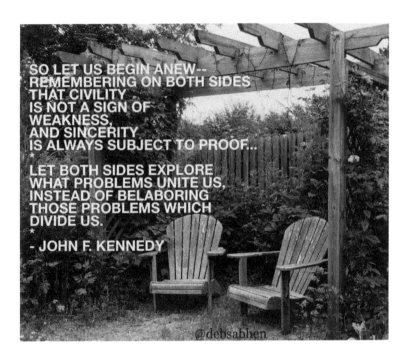

SO LET US BEGIN ANEW--
REMEMBERING ON BOTH SIDES
THAT CIVILITY
IS NOT A SIGN OF
WEAKNESS,
AND SINCERITY
IS ALWAYS SUBJECT TO PROOF...
*
LET BOTH SIDES EXPLORE
WHAT PROBLEMS UNITE US,
INSTEAD OF BELABORING
THOSE PROBLEMS WHICH
DIVIDE US.
*
- JOHN F. KENNEDY

@debsabhen

MISCOMMUNICATION LEADS TO COMPLICATION.
- LAURYN HILL
@debsabhen

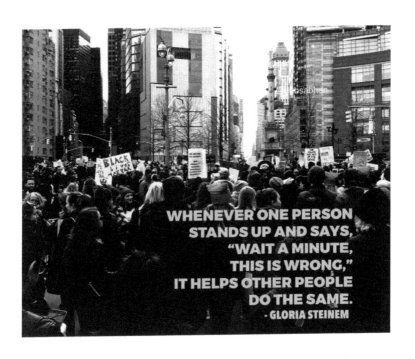

WHENEVER ONE PERSON
STANDS UP AND SAYS,
"WAIT A MINUTE,
THIS IS WRONG,"
IT HELPS OTHER PEOPLE
DO THE SAME.
- GLORIA STEINEM

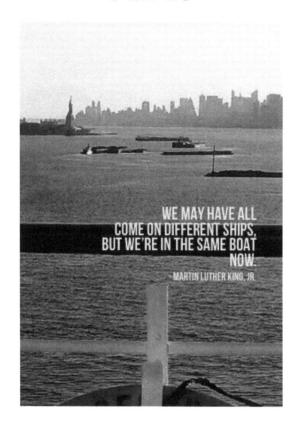

WE MAY HAVE ALL COME ON DIFFERENT SHIPS, BUT WE'RE IN THE SAME BOAT NOW.
- MARTIN LUTHER KING, JR.

THE ARC OF
THE MORAL UNIVERSE IS LONG,
BUT IT BENDS TOWARD JUSTICE.
- MARTIN LUTHER KING, JR

YOU CAN'T WAKE
A PERSON WHO IS PRETENDING
TO BE ASLEEP.
- NAVAJO PROVERB

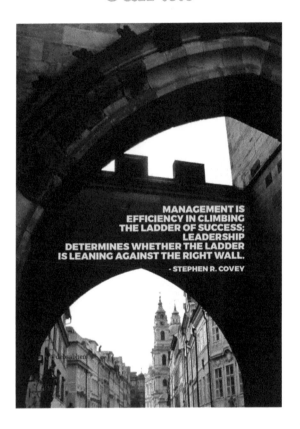

MANAGEMENT IS EFFICIENCY IN CLIMBING THE LADDER OF SUCCESS; LEADERSHIP DETERMINES WHETHER THE LADDER IS LEANING AGAINST THE RIGHT WALL.

- STEPHEN R. COVEY

MAKING THE SIMPLE
COMPLICATED
IS COMMONPLACE;
MAKING THE COMPLICATED
SIMPLE,
AWESOMELY SIMPLE,
THAT'S CREATIVITY.

- CHARLES MINGUS

@debsabhen

DON'T, LET SOMEONE DIM YOUR LIGHT, SIMPLY BECAUSE IT'S SHINING IN THEIR EYES.

—EDWARD DE BONO

@debsaukan

RAISE
YOUR WORDS,
NOT YOUR VOICE.
RAIN IS WHAT
GROWS FLOWERS,
NOT THUNDER.
- RUMI

. . . .

. . . .

. . . .

. . . .

. . . .

. . . .

WHAT GOOD
ARE WINGS
WITHOUT
THE
COURAGE
TO FLY?
– ATTICUS

@debsabhen

INTEGRITY, RESPECT, COMPASSION AND FAIRNESS BECOME OBSTACLES TO PEOPLE WHO THINK WINNING IS EVERYTHING.
- MICHAEL JOSEPHSON

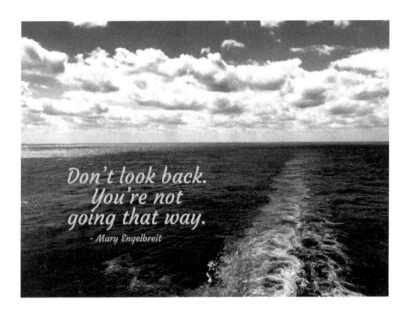

Don't look back.
You're not
going that way.
- Mary Engelbreit

HE WHO THINKS
HE IS
LEADING
BUT
HAS NO ONE
FOLLOWING HIM
IS ONLY
TAKING A WALK.
~ MALAWIAN PROVERB

@debsabhen

THE FURTHER A SOCIETY DRIFTS FROM TRUTH, THE MORE IT WILL HATE THOSE THAT SPEAK IT.

- GEORGE ORWELL

HATE:
IT HAS CAUSED
A LOT OF PROBLEMS
IN THIS WORLD,
BUT IT HAS NOT
SOLVED ONE YET
- MAYA ANGELOU

@debsabhen

IT TAKES MANY GOOD DEEDS
TO BUILD
A GOOD REPUTATION,
AND ONLY ONE BAD ONE
TO LOSE IT.
– BENJAMIN FRANKLIN

@debsabhen

LOSE AN HOUR IN THE MORNING,
AND YOU WILL BE ALL DAY
HUNTING FOR IT.
- RICHARD WHATELY

Feb 5

Feb 6

YOU MUST NEVER BE FEARFUL ABOUT WHAT YOU ARE DOING WHEN IT IS RIGHT.
- ROSA PARKS

....

....

....

....

....

....

THE BAD NEWS
IS TIME
FLIES.
THE GOOD NEWS
IS YOU'RE
THE PILOT.
- MICHAEL ALTSHULER

@debsabhen

YOU GROW UP
THE DAY YOU
HAVE YOUR FIRST
REAL LAUGH
AT YOURSELF.
- ETHEL BARRYMORE

PROGRESS IS IMPOSSIBLE
WITHOUT CHANGE;
AND THOSE WHO CANNOT
CHANGE THEIR MINDS,
CANNOT CHANGE
ANYTHING.
GEORGE BERNARD SHAW

CHANGING COURSE
CAN BE CHALLENGING,
BUT WHAT MAKES IT EXCITING
IS THE RESTORATION OF HOPE.
- THOMAS OPPONG

Feb 13

The most authentic
thing about us
is our capacity
to create,
to overcome,
to endure,
to transform,
to love and
to be greater
than our suffering.
— Ben Okri

. . . .

. . . .

. . . .

. . . .

. . . .

. . . .

Feb 14

51

OPTIMIST: SOMEONE WHO FIGURES THAT TAKING A STEP BACKWARD AFTER TAKING A STEP FORWARD IS NOT A DISASTER, IT'S A CHA-CHA.
- ROBERT BRAULT

APPRECIATION IS
A WONDERFUL THING:
IT MAKES WHAT IS
EXCELLENT IN OTHERS
BELONG TO US AS WELL.
- *Voltaire*

ACKNOWLEDGING
THE GOOD
THAT YOU ALREADY
HAVE IN YOUR LIFE
IS THE FOUNDATION
FOR ALL ABUNDANCE.
- ECKHART TOLLE

@debsabhen

Feb 18

NEARLY ALL MEN CAN STAND ADVERSITY; BUT IF YOU WANT TO TEST A MAN'S CHARACTER, GIVE HIM POWER.

- ROBERT G. INGERSOLL
(ABOUT ABRAHAM LINCOLN)

@deosabhen

. . . .

A MIND THAT IS STRETCHED BY A NEW EXPERIENCE CAN NEVER GO BACK TO ITS OLD DIMENSIONS.
- OLIVER WENDELL HOLMES, JR.

@debsabhen

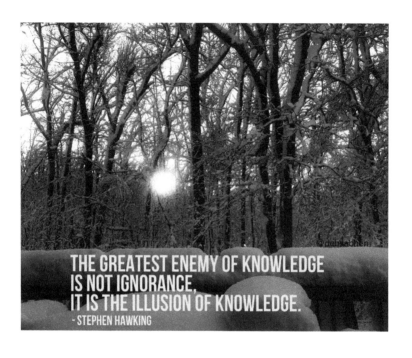

THE GREATEST ENEMY OF KNOWLEDGE
IS NOT IGNORANCE,
IT IS THE ILLUSION OF KNOWLEDGE.
- STEPHEN HAWKING

Feb 21

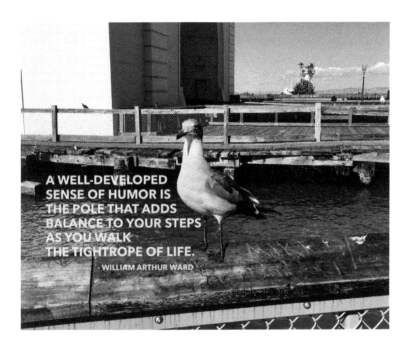

A WELL-DEVELOPED
SENSE OF HUMOR IS
THE POLE THAT ADDS
BALANCE TO YOUR STEPS
AS YOU WALK
THE TIGHTROPE OF LIFE.
- WILLIAM ARTHUR WARD

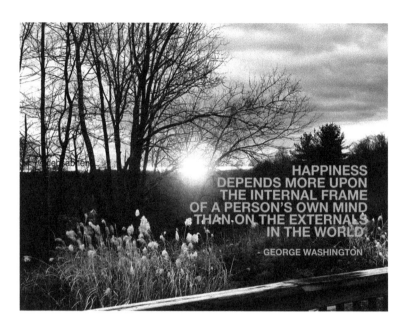

HAPPINESS
DEPENDS MORE UPON
THE INTERNAL FRAME
OF A PERSON'S OWN MIND
THAN ON THE EXTERNALS
IN THE WORLD.

- GEORGE WASHINGTON

THE HIGHEST FORM
OF IGNORANCE
IS WHEN YOU
REJECT SOMETHING
YOU DON'T KNOW
ANYTHING ABOUT.

- WAYNE DYER

@debsabhen

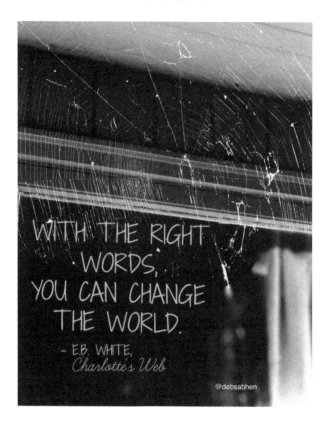

WITH THE RIGHT
WORDS,
YOU CAN CHANGE
THE WORLD.

– E.B. WHITE,
Charlotte's Web

@debsabhen

Feb 25

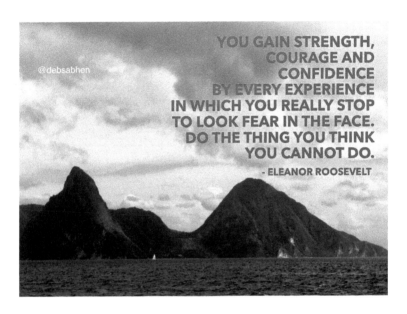

YOU GAIN STRENGTH,
COURAGE AND
CONFIDENCE
BY EVERY EXPERIENCE
IN WHICH YOU REALLY STOP
TO LOOK FEAR IN THE FACE.
DO THE THING YOU THINK
YOU CANNOT DO.

- ELEANOR ROOSEVELT

@debsabhen

IF YOU FIND
YOURSELF
IN A HOLE
STOP DIGGING.
- WILL ROGERS

@debsabhen

"If you don't want
anyone to...
find out,
Don't do it."

~ Chinese Proverb

@debsabhen

. . . .
. . . .
. . . .
. . . .
. . . .
. . . .

A GREAT MANY
PEOPLE THINK
THEY ARE
THINKING,
WHEN THEY ARE
MERELY
REARRANGING
THEIR PREJUDICES.

– WILLIAM JAMES

@debsablien

THERE WILL COME A TIME
WHEN YOU THINK EVERYTHING IS
FINISHED.
THAT WILL BE THE
BEGINNING.
—LOUIS L'AMOUR

THESE MOUNTAINS THAT YOU ARE CARRYING,
YOU WERE ONLY SUPPOSED TO CLIMB.
- NAJWA ZEBIAN

. . . .

. . . .

. . . .

. . . .

. . . .

. . . .

Create the life
you can't wait
to wake up to.
– Josie Spinardi

ADVICE
IS LIKE SNOW.
THE SOFTER IT FALLS,
THE LONGER
IT DWELLS UPON
AND THE DEEPER
IT SINKS INTO
THE MIND.
- SAMUEL TAYLOR COLERIDGE

IT'S HARD TO SEE THINGS
WHEN YOU'RE TOO CLOSE.
TAKE A STEP BACK
AND LOOK.
—Bob Ross

....
....
....
....
....
....

There is no force equal to a woman determined to rise.
~ W.E.B. DuBois

Mar 8

THERE'S A MOMENT
WHEN YOU HAVE TO
CHOOSE
WHETHER TO BE SILENT
OR TO STAND UP.
- MALALA YOUSAFZAI

. . . .

. . . .

. . . .

. . . .

. . . .

. . . .

AT SOME POINT,
YOU GOTTA LET GO,
AND SIT STILL,
AND ALLOW
CONTENTMENT
TO COME TO YOU.

- ELIZABETH GILBERT,
"EAT PRAY LOVE"

TRUTH WILL ALWAYS BE TRUTH,

REGARDLESS OF
LACK OF UNDERSTANDING,
DISBELIEF OR IGNORANCE.
W. CLEMENT STONE

IF YOU DON'T SEE
A CLEAR PATH
FOR WHAT YOU WANT,
SOMETIMES YOU HAVE TO
MAKE IT YOURSELF.
- MINDY KALING

IT IS TEMPTING, IF THE ONLY TOOL YOU HAVE IS A HAMMER, TO TREAT EVERYTHING AS IF IT WERE A NAIL.
- ABRAHAM MASLOW

THE TRUTH
WILL SET
YOU FREE,
BUT FIRST
IT WILL MAKE YOU
MISERABLE.
- JAMES A. GARFIELD

LIVE SO THAT WHEN
YOUR CHILDREN THINK OF
FAIRNESS, CARING AND INTEGRITY,
THEY THINK OF YOU.
- H. JACKSON BROWN, JR.

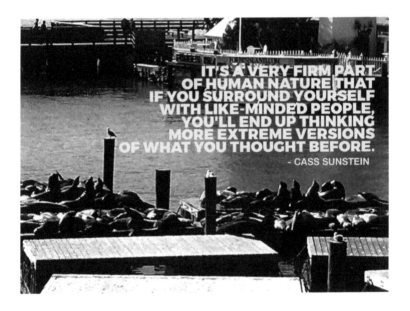

IT'S A VERY FIRM PART OF HUMAN NATURE THAT IF YOU SURROUND YOURSELF WITH LIKE-MINDED PEOPLE, YOU'LL END UP THINKING MORE EXTREME VERSIONS OF WHAT YOU THOUGHT BEFORE.

- CASS SUNSTEIN

SOMETIMES
IN THE WAVES
OF CHANGE,
WE FIND
OUR TRUE DIRECTION.

- ANONYMOUS

@debsabhen

YOU GOTTA TRY YOUR LUCK
AT LEAST ONCE A DAY,
BECAUSE YOU COULD BE
GOING AROUND
LUCKY ALL DAY
AND NOT EVEN KNOW IT.
- JIMMY DEAN

Mar 18

THE DIFFICULT
I'LL DO RIGHT NOW.
THE IMPOSSIBLE
WILL TAKE
A LITTLE WHILE.
- BILLIE HOLIDAY

MEETINGS ARE INDISPENSABLE WHEN YOU DON'T WANT TO DO ANYTHING.

– JOHN KENNETH GALBRAITH

IT IS A SIGN OF GREAT
INNER INSECURITY
TO BE HOSTILE TO
THE UNFAMILIAR.
- ANAÏS NIN

@debsabhen

GO LOOKING FOR THE BEST IN PEOPLE AND YOU'LL BE AMAZED AT HOW MUCH TALENT, INGENUITY, EMPATHY AND GOOD YOU WILL FIND.

- BOB BURG

@debsabhen

JUSTICE CONSISTS NOT IN BEING NEUTRAL BETWEEN RIGHT AND WRONG, BUT IN FINDING OUT THE RIGHT AND UPHOLDING IT, WHEREVER FOUND, AGAINST THE WRONG.
- THEODORE ROOSEVELT

@debsabhen

**Never limit yourself
because of others'
limited imagination;
Never limit others
because of your own
limited imagination.**

- Mae Jemison, Astronaut

....

....

....

....

....

....

COULD A GREATER MIRACLE
TAKE PLACE THAN TO
LOOK THROUGH EACH OTHER'S EYES
FOR AN INSTANT?
– HENRY DAVID THOREAU

BE WILLING TO BE
A BEGINNER EVERY
SINGLE MORNING.
- MEISTER ECKHART

@debsabhen

PERCEPTION
IS REAL,
EVEN WHEN IT IS NOT
REALITY.
- EDWARD DE BONO -

@debsabhen

IT TAKES
NO MORE TIME
TO SEE
THE GOOD SIDE
OF LIFE
THAN TO SEE
THE BAD.
- JIMMY BUFFETT

THE MOMENT A PERSON FORMS A THEORY, HIS IMAGINATION SEES IN EVERY OBJECT ONLY THE TRAITS WHICH FAVOR THAT THEORY. THOMAS JEFFERSON

THE BEST WAY TO
PERSUADE PEOPLE
IS WITH YOUR EARS—
BY LISTENING TO THEM.

- DEAN RUSK

PROGRESS LIES NOT IN
ENHANCING WHAT IS,
BUT IN ADVANCING TOWARD
WHAT WILL BE.
– KHALIL GIBRAN

FOR
FAST-ACTING
RELIEF,
TRY SLOWING DOWN.
- LILY TOMLIN

@debsabhen

Apr 1

THERE'S NO HARM IN HOPING FOR THE BEST, AS LONG AS YOU'RE PREPARED FOR THE WORST.
- STEPHEN KING

Apr 2

KINDNESS IS IN OUR POWER,
EVEN WHEN FONDNESS IS NOT.
- SAMUEL JOHNSON

....

....

....

....

....

....

**FAILURE IS A PREREQUISITE
FOR GREAT SUCCESS.
IF YOU WANT TO SUCCEED FASTER,
DOUBLE YOUR RATE OF FAILURE.**

- BRIAN TRACY

....

....

....

....

....

....

Trust
is built
in very
small moments.
— Brené Brown

@debsabhen

Apr 5

PERSPECTIVE
IS THE WAY WE SEE THINGS
WHEN WE LOOK AT THEM
FROM A CERTAIN DISTANCE,
AND IT ALLOWS US TO APPRECIATE
THEIR TRUE VALUE.

- RAFAEL E. PINO

BE YOURSELF.
NO ONE CAN EVER TELL YOU
YOU'RE DOING IT WRONG.
- JAMES LEO HERLIHY

Patience
is a form of wisdom.
It demonstrates
that we understand and
accept the fact that
sometimes things must unfold
in their own time.

- Jon Kabat-Zinn

@debsabhen

Sometimes you will never know the value of a moment until it becomes a memory.
— Theodore "Dr." Seuss Geisel

@debsabhen

There is freedom
waiting for you
on the breezes
of the sky.
And you ask,
"What if I fall?"
Oh, but my darling,
what if you fly?

- Erin Hanson

Storms make trees take deeper roots.
- Dolly Parton

@debsabhen

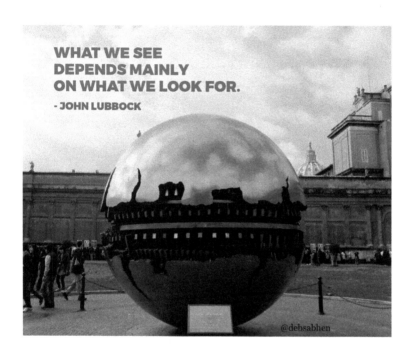

WHAT WE SEE
DEPENDS MAINLY
ON WHAT WE LOOK FOR.
- JOHN LUBBOCK

@debsabhen

Time heals what
Reason cannot.

– Seneca

@debsabben

The deepest principle in human nature
is the craving to be appreciated.

- William James

THE GREATEST GOOD
YOU CAN DO FOR ANOTHER
IS NOT JUST TO
SHARE YOUR RICHES,
BUT TO REVEAL
TO HIM HIS OWN.
- BENJAMIN DISRAELI

YOUR VISION IS ONLY ACTIONABLE
IF YOU SAY IT OUT LOUD.
IF YOU KEEP IT TO YOURSELF,
IT WILL REMAIN A FIGMENT
OF YOUR IMAGINATION. @debsabhen
- SIMON SINEK

....

....

....

....

....

....

THERE'S ALWAYS TOMORROW
TO START OVER AGAIN
THINGS WILL NEVER STAY THE SAME
THE ONLY ONE SURE THING IS CHANGE
THAT'S WHY THERE'S ALWAYS TOMORROW
- GLORIA ESTEFAN

Forgive yourself for not having
the foresight to know
what now seems
so obvious in hindsight.
- Judy Belmont

@debsabhen

A TREE THAT IS UNBENDING IS EASILY BROKEN.
- LAO TZU

THE ONLY THING
NECESSARY
FOR EVIL
TO TRIUMPH
IS FOR GOOD MEN
TO DO
NOTHING.
- EDMUND BURKE

IF YOU WATCH HOW NATURE DEALS WITH ADVERSITY, CONTINUALLY RENEWING ITSELF, YOU CAN'T HELP BUT LEARN.

- BERNIE SIEGEL

SCATTER
JOY.
- RALPH WALDO EMERSON
@debsabhen

Try to leave the Earth
a little better than when you arrived.

Sidney Sheldon

Apr 23

TREAT THE EARTH WELL.
IT WAS NOT GIVEN TO YOU
BY YOUR PARENTS;
IT WAS LOANED TO YOU
BY YOUR CHILDREN...
- NATIVE AMERICAN PROVERB

OLD MINDS
ARE LIKE OLD HORSES;
YOU MUST EXERCISE THEM,
IF YOU WISH TO KEEP THEM
IN WORKING ORDER.
- JOHN ADAMS

@debsabhen

WAITING FOR PERFECT IS NEVER AS SMART AS MAKING PROGRESS.
—SETH GODIN

Most people never run
far enough on their
first wind
to find out they've
got a second.

~William James

BE A GOOD
LISTENER.
YOUR EARS
WILL NEVER GET YOU
IN TROUBLE.
- FRANK TYGER

@debsabhen

AS WE WORK
TO CREATE
LIGHT
FOR
OTHERS,
WE
NATURALLY
LIGHT
OUR OWN WAY.
- Mary Anne Radmacher

@debsabhen

Apr 29

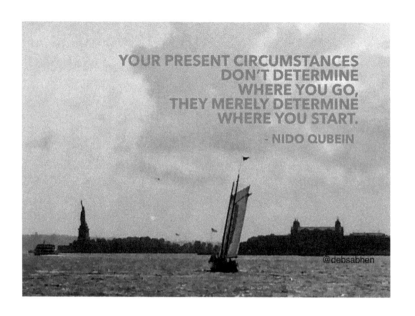

YOUR PRESENT CIRCUMSTANCES
DON'T DETERMINE
WHERE YOU GO,
THEY MERELY DETERMINE
WHERE YOU START.

- NIDO QUBEIN

@debsabhen

....

....

....

....

....

....

MISTAKES ARE THE PORTALS OF DISCOVERY.

- JAMES JOYCE

@debsabhen

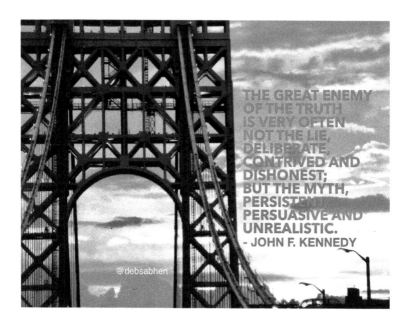

THE GREAT ENEMY
OF THE TRUTH
IS VERY OFTEN
NOT THE LIE,
DELIBERATE,
CONTRIVED AND
DISHONEST;
BUT THE MYTH,
PERSISTENT,
PERSUASIVE AND
UNREALISTIC.
- JOHN F. KENNEDY

@debsabhen

@debsabhen

THE BEGINNING
IS THE MOST
IMPORTANT PART
OF THE WORK.
- PLATO

A WOODPECKER CAN TAP TWENTY TIMES
ON A THOUSAND TREES
AND GET NOWHERE, BUT STAY BUSY.
OR HE CAN TAP TWENTY-THOUSAND TIMES
ON ONE TREE
AND GET DINNER.
- SETH GODIN

@debsabhen

NEVER GIVE UP,
FOR THAT IS JUST THE TIME
WHEN THE TIDE WILL TURN.
- HARRIET BEECHER STOWE

Tomorrow
is a new day,
with no mistakes
in it yet.
- L.M. Montgomery,
"Anne Of Green Gables"

May 6

FOCUS
IS DECIDING
WHAT THINGS
YOU'RE
NOT
GOING TO DO.
— JOHN CARMACK

@debsabhen

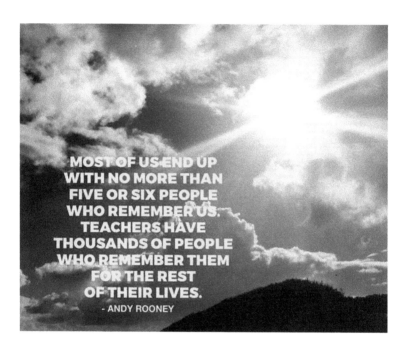

MOST OF US END UP
WITH NO MORE THAN
FIVE OR SIX PEOPLE
WHO REMEMBER US.
TEACHERS HAVE
THOUSANDS OF PEOPLE
WHO REMEMBER THEM
FOR THE REST
OF THEIR LIVES.
- ANDY ROONEY

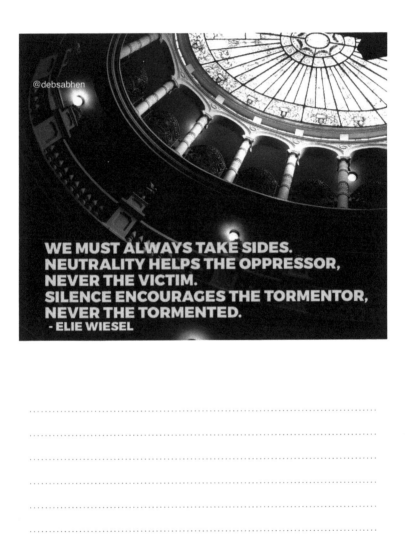

@debsabhen

WE MUST ALWAYS TAKE SIDES.
NEUTRALITY HELPS THE OPPRESSOR,
NEVER THE VICTIM.
SILENCE ENCOURAGES THE TORMENTOR,
NEVER THE TORMENTED.
- ELIE WIESEL

A LIE HAS SPEED,
BUT TRUTH
HAS ENDURANCE.
— EDGAR J. MOHN

Publicity
is justly commended for
social and industrial diseases.
Sunlight
is said to be the best of
disinfectants;
Electric light
the most efficient
policeman.

- Justice Louis D. Brandeis

May 11

Nothing is worth more than this day.
You cannot relive yesterday.
Tomorrow is still
beyond your reach.
~Johann Wolfgang Von Goethe

@debsabhan

May 12

@debsabhen

HERE'S TO STRONG
WOMEN.
MAY WE KNOW THEM.
MAY WE BE THEM.
MAY WE
RAISE THEM.

UNKNOWN

May 13

PERSEVERANCE
IS FAILING
19 TIMES
AND
SUCCEEDING
THE 20TH.
- JULIE ANDREWS

@debsabhen

THE COURAGE OF LEADERSHIP
IS GIVING OTHERS
THE CHANCE TO SUCCEED,
EVEN THOUGH YOU
BEAR THE RESPONSIBILITY
FOR GETTING THINGS
DONE.

- SIMON SINEK

ABILITY IS IMPORTANT IN OUR
QUEST FOR SUCCESS,
BUT DEPENDABILITY IS CRITICAL.
- ZIG ZIGLAR

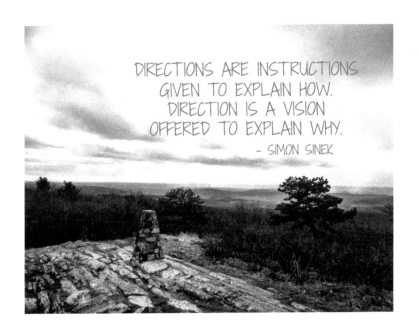

DIRECTIONS ARE INSTRUCTIONS
GIVEN TO EXPLAIN HOW.
DIRECTION IS A VISION
OFFERED TO EXPLAIN WHY.
- SIMON SINEK

THERE COMES A DAY WHEN
YOU REALIZE TURNING THE PAGE
IS THE BEST FEELING
IN THE WORLD,
BECAUSE YOU REALIZE
THERE'S SO MUCH MORE
TO THE BOOK
THAN THE PAGE
YOU WERE STUCK ON.

@debsabben

....

....

....

....

....

....

May 18

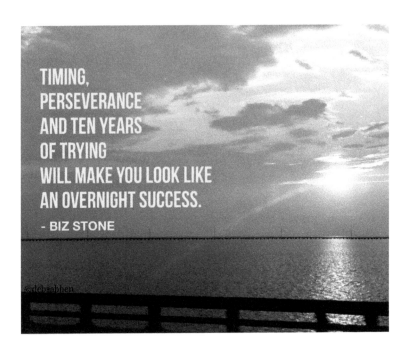

TIMING,
PERSEVERANCE
AND TEN YEARS
OF TRYING
WILL MAKE YOU LOOK LIKE
AN OVERNIGHT SUCCESS.

- BIZ STONE

@debsabben

REMEMBER.. YOU'RE BRAVER THAN YOU BELIEVE, STRONGER THAN YOU SEEM, AND SMARTER THAN YOU THINK.
- A.A. MILNE, *Winnie-the-Pooh*

@debsabhen

May 20

It's the possibility of having a dream come true that makes life interesting.

Paulo Coelho

There is a
difference
between truly
listening
and
waiting for
your turn
to talk.
- Ralph Waldo Emerson
@debsabhen

A SHIP IN PORT IS SAFE,
BUT THAT IS NOT WHAT
SHIPS ARE BUILT FOR.
SAIL OUT TO SEA
AND DO NEW THINGS.

- RADM. GRACE M. HOPPER, USN,
COMPUTER SCIENCE PIONEER

LET US BE
GRATEFUL
TO THE PEOPLE
WHO MAKE US
HAPPY.
THEY ARE THE
CHARMING
GARDENERS
WHO MAKE
OUR SOULS
BLOSSOM.

MARCEL PROUST

A PEOPLE THAT
VALUES
ITS PRIVILEGES
ABOVE
ITS PRINCIPLES
SOON LOSES BOTH.

- Dwight D. Eisenhower

@debsabhen

A PERSON OFTEN MEETS
HIS DESTINY
ON THE ROAD HE TOOK
TO AVOID IT.
- JEAN DE LA FONTAINE

@debsabhen

MEASURE YOUR IMPACT
ON HUMANITY
NOT IN LIKES,
BUT BY THE LIVES
YOU TOUCH.
NOT ON POPULARITY,
BUT BY THE PEOPLE
YOU SERVE.

- TIM COOK
(MIT COMMENCEMENT SPEECH)

May 27

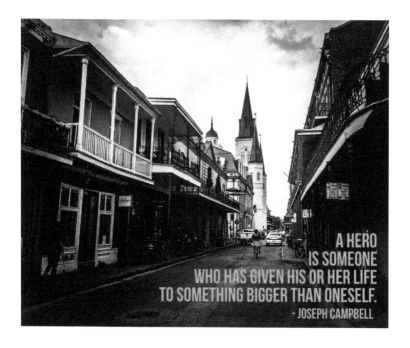

A HERO IS SOMEONE WHO HAS GIVEN HIS OR HER LIFE TO SOMETHING BIGGER THAN ONESELF.
- JOSEPH CAMPBELL

Our greatest glory
is not
in never falling,
but in rising
every time we fall.
– Confucius

@debsabhan

@debsabhen

The cure for
anything
is salt water.
Sweat,
tears
or the sea.

~ Isak Dinesen

....
....
....
....
....
....

BEFORE I CAN LIVE WITH
OTHER FOLKS,
I'VE GOT TO LIVE WITH
MYSELF.
THE ONE THING
THAT DOESN'T ABIDE
BY MAJORITY RULE
IS A PERSON'S
CONSCIENCE.

- ATTICUS FINCH IN
"TO KILL A MOCKINGBIRD,"
BY HARPER LEE

THE
MOST
PRECIOUS
GIFT
WE CAN
OFFER
OTHERS IS
OUR PRESENCE.
- NHAT HANH

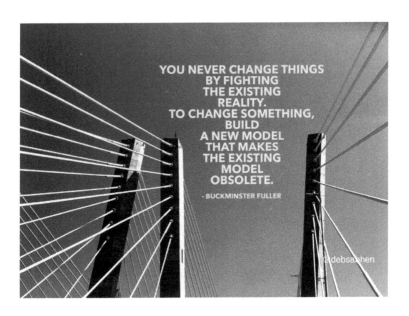

YOU NEVER CHANGE THINGS
BY FIGHTING
THE EXISTING
REALITY.
TO CHANGE SOMETHING,
BUILD
A NEW MODEL
THAT MAKES
THE EXISTING
MODEL
OBSOLETE.

- BUCKMINSTER FULLER

@debsanhen

WISE MEN TALK
BECAUSE THEY HAVE
SOMETHING TO SAY.
FOOLS,
BECAUSE THEY HAVE
TO SAY SOMETHING.

- PLATO

AN OPTIMIST
IS THE HUMAN
PERSONIFICATION
OF SPRING.
- SUSAN J. BISSONETTE

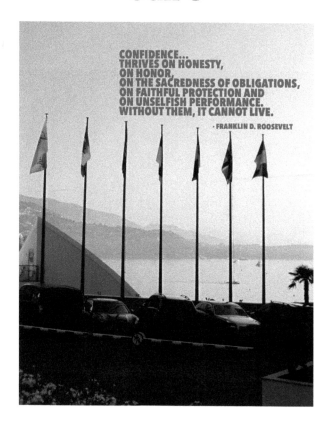

CONFIDENCE...
THRIVES ON HONESTY,
ON HONOR,
ON THE SACREDNESS OF OBLIGATIONS,
ON FAITHFUL PROTECTION AND
ON UNSELFISH PERFORMANCE.
WITHOUT THEM, IT CANNOT LIVE.

- FRANKLIN D. ROOSEVELT

POWER,
AT ITS BEST,
IS LOVE
IMPLEMENTING
THE DEMAND OF JUSTICE.
– Martin Luther King Jr.

Jun 8

THE REALLY HAPPY PERSON
IS THE ONE WHO CAN ENJOY THE SCENERY,
EVEN WHEN THEY HAVE TO TAKE A DETOUR.
- JAMES JEANS

@debsabhen

DON'T JUDGE
EACH DAY
BY THE HARVEST
YOU REAP,
BUT BY THE SEEDS
YOU PLANT.

- ROBERT LOUIS STEVENSON

@debsauhen

If you don't know where
you are going,
any road will get you there.
– Lewis Carroll,
"Alice in Wonderland"

@gebsabbun

If you want the cooperation of humans around you, you must make them feel they are important—and you do that by being genuine and humble.
– Nelson Mandela

IN LIFE,
CHANGE IS
INEVITABLE.
IN BUSINESS,
CHANGE IS
VITAL.
- WARREN BENNIS

WE ARE MASTERS OF
THE UNSAID WORDS,
BUT SLAVES OF
THOSE WE
LET SLIP OUT.

- WINSTON CHURCHILL

SOMETIMES
THE ONLY REASON
FOR US TO BE
SOMEWHERE ELSE
IS TO SEE THINGS FROM
A DIFFERENT PERSPECTIVE.

- LEILA SUMMERS

....
....
....
....
....
....

THOUSANDS OF CANDLES
CAN BE LIT FROM
ONE SINGLE CANDLE,
AND THE LIFE
OF THE CANDLE
IS NOT SHORTENED...
HAPPINESS
NEVER DECREASES
BY BEING SHARED.

*the Buddha,
Siddhartha Guatama*

ATTENTION IS THE RAREST AND PUREST FORM OF GENEROSITY.
— SIMONE WEIL

@daysanhen

....

....

....

....

....

EVEN IF YOU'RE
ON THE RIGHT TRACK,
YOU'LL GET RUN OVER
IF YOU JUST SIT THERE.
- WILL ROGERS

@debsabhen

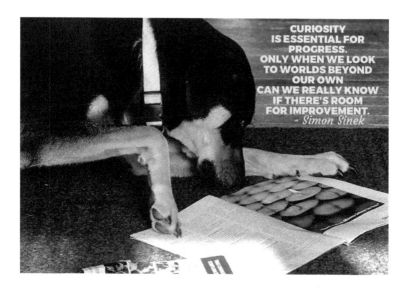

CURIOSITY
IS ESSENTIAL FOR
PROGRESS.
ONLY WHEN WE LOOK
TO WORLDS BEYOND
OUR OWN
CAN WE REALLY KNOW
IF THERE'S ROOM
FOR IMPROVEMENT.
- Simon Sinek

IN AN ORGANIZATION
WHERE TRUST
AND THE
DIGNITY OF INDIVIDUALS
ARE HELD AS
THE HIGHEST VALUES,
SHAME AND BLAME
DON'T WORK AS
MANAGEMENT STYLES.

- BRENÉ BROWN

BECOME SO WRAPPED UP IN SOMETHING THAT YOU FORGET TO BE AFRAID.

- LADY BIRD JOHNSON

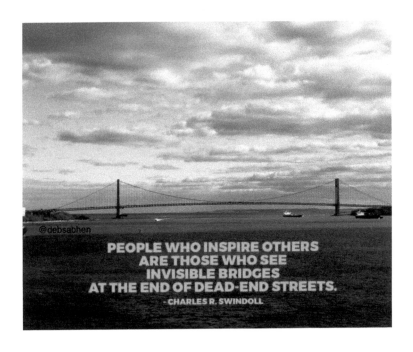

@debsabhen

**PEOPLE WHO INSPIRE OTHERS
ARE THOSE WHO SEE
INVISIBLE BRIDGES
AT THE END OF DEAD-END STREETS.**
- CHARLES R. SWINDOLL

@debsabhen

WHEREVER
YOU ARE,
BE ALL THERE.

- JIM ELLIOT

In matters of style,
swim with the current;
In matters of principle,
stand like a rock.
—Thomas Jefferson

@debsabhen

. . . .

. . . .

. . . .

. . . .

. . . .

Never lose sight of the fact
that the most important
yardstick of your success
will be how you treat other people.
- Barbara Bush

LEADERSHIP IS ABOUT MAKING OTHERS BETTER AS A RESULT OF YOUR PRESENCE AND MAKING SURE THAT IMPACT LASTS IN YOUR ABSENCE.
- UNKNOWN

@debsabhen

When you live on a round planet,
there's no choosing sides.
- Wayne Dyer

CHILDREN ARE HUMAN BEINGS TO WHOM RESPECT IS DUE, SUPERIOR TO US BY REASON OF THEIR INNOCENCE AND OF THE GREATER POSSIBILITIES OF THEIR FUTURE.
- MARIA MONTESSORI

@debsabhen

SHE STOOD IN THE STORM,
AND WHEN THE WIND
DID NOT BLOW HER WAY...
SHE ADJUSTED HER SAILS.

- ELIZABETH EDWARDS

Jun 30

I THINK WE ALL HAVE EMPATHY. WE MAY NOT HAVE ENOUGH COURAGE TO DISPLAY IT [HOWEVER].

- MAYA ANGELOU

DIPLOMACY IS MORE THAN SAYING OR DOING THE RIGHT THINGS AT THE RIGHT TIME; IT IS AVOIDING SAYING OR DOING THE WRONG THINGS AT ANY TIME.

- BO BENNETT

Children are the living messages we send to a time we cannot see.
— Neil Postman

May we think of freedom,
not as the right
to do as we please,
but as the opportunity
to do what is right.
- Peter Marshall

Jul 4

...SILENT LIPS.
"GIVE ME YOUR TIRED, YOUR POOR,
YOUR HUDDLED MASSES YEARNING TO BREATHE FREE,
THE WRETCHED REFUSE OF YOUR TEEMING SHORE.
SEND THESE, THE HOMELESS, TEMPEST-TOST TO ME,
I LIFT MY LAMP BESIDE THE GOLDEN DOOR!"

HERE AT OUR SEA-WASHED, SUNSET GATES
SHALL STAND
A MIGHTY WOMAN
WITH A TORCH,
WHOSE FLAME IS
THE IMPRISONED
LIGHTNING,
AND HER NAME
MOTHER OF EXILES.
FROM HER BEACON-HAND
GLOWS WORLD-WIDE WELCOME...

- EMMA LAZARUS,
"THE NEW COLOSSUS,"
(SONNET FOR THE
STATUE OF LIBERTY, 1883)

The hard part of a revolution is not making a revolution, it's implementing its goals.

- John McCain

Almost everything
will work again
if you unplug it
for a few minutes...
including you.
– Anne Lamott

TODAY IS ONLY ONE DAY
IN ALL THE DAYS THAT WILL EVER BE.
BUT WHAT WILL HAPPEN
IN ALL THE DAYS THAT WILL EVER COME
CAN DEPEND ON
WHAT YOU DO TODAY.

- ERNEST HEMINGWAY
"FOR WHOM THE BELLS TOLL"

NEVER DOUBT
THAT A GROUP OF THOUGHTFUL,
COMMITTED CITIZENS
CAN CHANGE THE WORLD.
INDEED,
IT IS THE ONLY THING
THAT EVER HAS.
- MARGARET MEAD

THE PURPOSE OF LIFE
IS TO DISCOVER
YOUR GIFT.
THE WORK OF LIFE
IS TO DEVELOP IT.
THE MEANING OF LIFE
IS TO GIVE IT AWAY.
- DAVID VISCOTT

@debsabhen

YOU ARE NEVER TOO OLD TO SET ANOTHER GOAL OR TO DREAM A NEW DREAM.
- C.S. LEWIS

@debsabhen

PEACE IS MORE THAN JUST AN ABSENCE OF WAR. TRUE PEACE IS JUSTICE, TRUE PEACE IS FREEDOM, AND TRUE PEACE DICTATES THE RECOGNITION OF HUMAN RIGHTS.

- RONALD REAGAN

@debsabnen

COMPASSION
IS THE
KEEN AWARENESS
OF THE
INTERDEPENDENCE
OF ALL THINGS.
- THOMAS MERTON

WISDOM TOO OFTEN NEVER COMES,
SO ONE OUGHT NOT TO DISMISS IT
MERELY BECAUSE IT COMES LATE.

- FELIX FRANKFURTER

One of the secrets of life is that all that is really worth the doing is what we do for others.
— Lewis Carroll, *Alice in Wonderland*

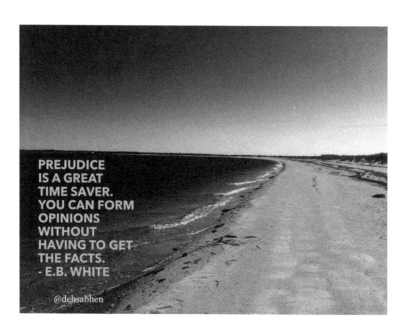

PREJUDICE
IS A GREAT
TIME SAVER.
YOU CAN FORM
OPINIONS
WITHOUT
HAVING TO GET
THE FACTS.
- E.B. WHITE

@debsabhen

DON'T TELL
ME THE SKY'S
THE LIMIT
WHEN THERE
ARE FOOTPRINTS
ON THE MOON.

- PAUL BRANDT

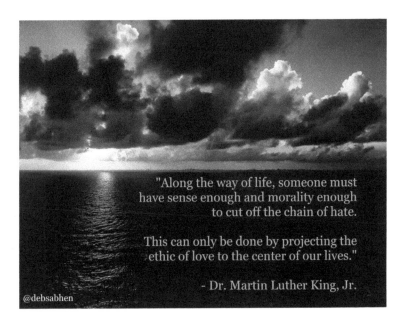

"Along the way of life, someone must have sense enough and morality enough to cut off the chain of hate.

This can only be done by projecting the ethic of love to the center of our lives."

- Dr. Martin Luther King, Jr.

@debsabhen

YOUR ASSUMPTIONS
ARE YOUR WINDOWS ON THE WORLD.
SCRUB THEM OFF EVERY ONCE IN AWHILE,
OR THE LIGHT WON'T COME IN.
- ALAN ALDA

COMMITMENT TO THE RULE OF LAW PROVIDES A BASIC ASSURANCE THAT PEOPLE CAN KNOW WHAT TO EXPECT, WHETHER WHAT THEY DO IS POPULAR OR UNPOPULAR AT THE TIME.

– SANDRA DAY O'CONNOR

Jul 25

THE MOMENT A PERSON FORMS A THEORY, HIS IMAGINATION SEES IN EVERY OBJECT ONLY THE TRAITS WHICH FAVOR THAT THEORY.
-THOMAS JEFFERSON

A SUCCESSFUL MAN
IS ONE WHO CAN
LAY A FIRM
FOUNDATION
FROM THE BRICKS
OTHERS HAVE THROWN
AT HIM.
- DAVID BRINKLEY

WE'RE SO BUSY
WATCHING OUT FOR
WHAT'S JUST AHEAD OF US,
THAT WE DON'T
TAKE TIME TO ENJOY
WHERE WE ARE.

- BILL WATTERSON

Jul 28

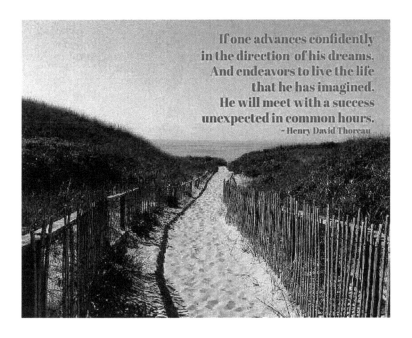

If one advances confidently
in the direction of his dreams,
And endeavors to live the life
that he has imagined,
He will meet with a success
unexpected in common hours.
- Henry David Thoreau

IT IS BETTER TO FAIL IN ORIGINALITY
THAN TO SUCCEED IN IMITATION.
– HERMAN MELVILLE

@debsabhen

IT IS NOT THE
STRONGEST
SPECIES
THAT SURVIVE,
NOR THE MOST
INTELLIGENT,
BUT THE MOST
RESPONSIVE TO CHANGE.
- CHARLES DARWIN
<AS PARAPHRASED BY
PROF. LEON C. MEGGINSON>

PATIENCE IS NOT SIMPLY
THE ABILITY TO WAIT—
IT'S HOW WE BEHAVE
WHILE WE'RE WAITING.

- JOYCE MEYER

Aug 1

IF YOU THINK
IT'S EXPENSIVE
TO HIRE A PROFESSIONAL TO
DO THE JOB,
WAIT UNTIL YOU HIRE
AN AMATEUR.
- Red Adair

STAY OPTIMISTIC
TO THE POINT WHERE
PEOPLE QUESTION
YOUR SANITY.

- MATTHEW BARNETT

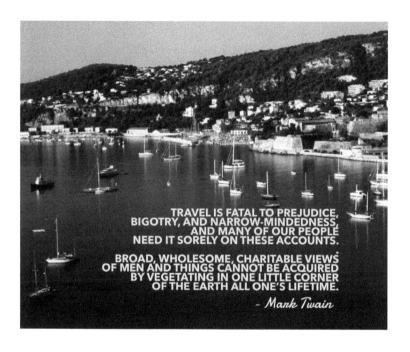

TRAVEL IS FATAL TO PREJUDICE, BIGOTRY, AND NARROW-MINDEDNESS, AND MANY OF OUR PEOPLE NEED IT SORELY ON THESE ACCOUNTS.

BROAD, WHOLESOME, CHARITABLE VIEWS OF MEN AND THINGS CANNOT BE ACQUIRED BY VEGETATING IN ONE LITTLE CORNER OF THE EARTH ALL ONE'S LIFETIME.

– Mark Twain

Aug 4

What is done cannot be undone,
but one can prevent it happening again.
- Anne Frank

@debsabhen

IF YOU THINK
YOU ARE TOO SMALL
TO MAKE
A DIFFERENCE,
TRY SLEEPING
WITH A
MOSQUITO.

- DALAI LAMA XIV

IF YOU ARE FREE,
YOU NEED TO FREE SOMEBODY ELSE.
IF YOU HAVE SOME POWER,
THEN YOUR JOB IS TO EMPOWER
SOMEBODY ELSE.
— TONI MORRISON

Aug 7

225

IF YOU DISRESPECT EVERYBODY YOU RUN INTO, HOW IN THE WORLD DO YOU THINK EVERYBODY'S SUPPOSED TO RESPECT YOU?

-ARETHA FRANKLIN

There is more to life
than increasing its speed.
-Mohandas K. Gandhi

Tell the truth,
or someone
will tell it
for you.
~ Stephanie Klein

. . . .

. . . .

. . . .

. . . .

. . . .

. . . .

TRUST
YOUR OWN
INSTINCTS.
YOUR
MISTAKES
MIGHT AS WELL
BE YOUR OWN,
INSTEAD OF
SOMEONE ELSE'S.

- BILLY WILDER

@debsabhen

Aug 14

Most people just laugh when they hear that the secret to success is giving.
Then again, most people are nowhere near as successful as they wish they were.

-Bob Burg

Never be bullied
into silence.
Never allow yourself
to be made a victim.
Accept no one's
definition
of your life;
Define yourself.

– Harvey Fierstein

The world
is changed by
your example,
not by
your opinion.
- Paulo Coelho

@debsabhen

WHEN THE POWER OF LOVE
OVERCOMES THE LOVE OF POWER,
THE WORLD WILL KNOW PEACE.
- JIMI HENDRIX
(PARAPHRASING SRI CHINMOY)

A party without a cake
is just a meeting.
- Julia Child

WHEN YOU HAVE THE CHOICE BETWEEN BEING RIGHT AND BEING KIND, JUST CHOOSE KIND.

~WAYNE DYER

@debsabhen

WHEN YOU
FORGIVE,
YOU IN NO WAY
CHANGE THE PAST;
BUT YOU SURE DO
CHANGE THE FUTURE.

- BERNARD MELTZER

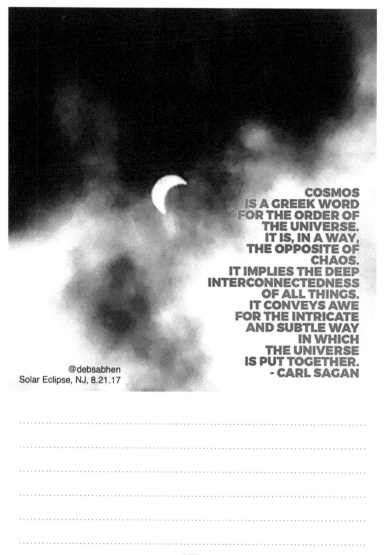

COSMOS IS A GREEK WORD FOR THE ORDER OF THE UNIVERSE. IT IS, IN A WAY, THE OPPOSITE OF CHAOS. IT IMPLIES THE DEEP INTERCONNECTEDNESS OF ALL THINGS. IT CONVEYS AWE FOR THE INTRICATE AND SUBTLE WAY IN WHICH THE UNIVERSE IS PUT TOGETHER.
- CARL SAGAN

@debsabhen
Solar Eclipse, NJ, 8.21.17

THE GREATEST
THREAT TO OUR PLANET
IS THE BELIEF THAT SOMEONE ELSE
WILL SAVE IT.

- ROBERT SWAN

Aug 23

Some beautiful paths
can't be discovered
without getting
lost.
–Erol Ozan

....
....
....
....
....
....

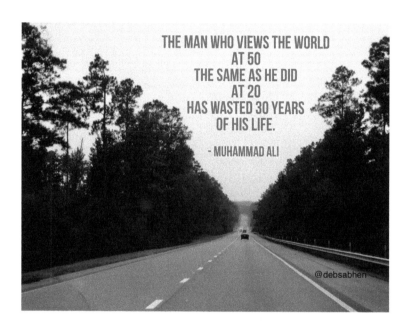

THE MAN WHO VIEWS THE WORLD
AT 50
THE SAME AS HE DID
AT 20
HAS WASTED 30 YEARS
OF HIS LIFE.

- MUHAMMAD ALI

@debsabhen

....

....

....

....

....

....

A PERSON OFTEN MEETS
HIS DESTINY
ON THE ROAD HE TOOK
TO AVOID IT.
- JEAN DE LA FONTAINE

@debsabhen

A HEALTHY VISION
OF THE FUTURE
IS NOT POSSIBLE WITHOUT
AN ACCURATE KNOWLEDGE
OF THE PAST.
- DAISAKU IKEDA

@debsabbey

MISTAKES
ARE THE USUAL BRIDGE
BETWEEN
INEXPERIENCE AND WISDOM.
- PHYLLIS THEROUX

IT AIN'T WHAT
YOU DON'T KNOW
THAT GETS YOU INTO TROUBLE;
IT'S WHAT YOU KNOW
FOR SURE
THAT JUST AIN'T SO.

—MARK TWAIN

THERE ARE
NO WRONG
TURNINGS,
ONLY
PATHS
WE HAD
NOT KNOWN
WE WERE
MEANT TO WALK.
- GUY GAVRIEL KAY,
FROM "TIGANA"

@debsabhen

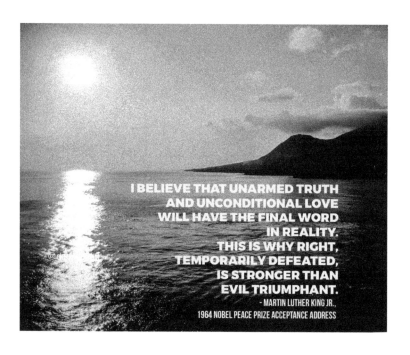

I BELIEVE THAT UNARMED TRUTH
AND UNCONDITIONAL LOVE
WILL HAVE THE FINAL WORD
IN REALITY.
THIS IS WHY RIGHT,
TEMPORARILY DEFEATED,
IS STRONGER THAN
EVIL TRIUMPHANT.
- MARTIN LUTHER KING JR.,
1964 NOBEL PEACE PRIZE ACCEPTANCE ADDRESS

Summer's lease
hath all too
short a date.
—William Shakespeare

WHEN YOU DON'T KNOW WHAT TO EXPECT,
PREPARE FOR THE UNEXPECTED.
- PIERRE OMIDYAR

IN MOST CASES,
BEING A
GOOD BOSS
MEANS HIRING
TALENTED PEOPLE
AND THEN GETTING
OUT OF THEIR WAY.
– Tina Fey

Inspiration exists,
but it has to find you working.
- Pablo Picasso

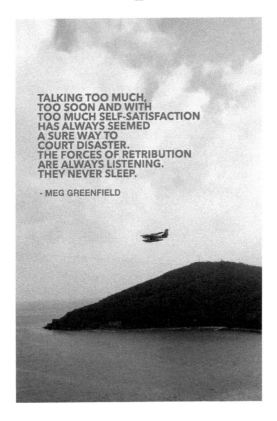

TALKING TOO MUCH,
TOO SOON AND WITH
TOO MUCH SELF-SATISFACTION
HAS ALWAYS SEEMED
A SURE WAY TO
COURT DISASTER.
THE FORCES OF RETRIBUTION
ARE ALWAYS LISTENING.
THEY NEVER SLEEP.

- MEG GREENFIELD

Sep 6

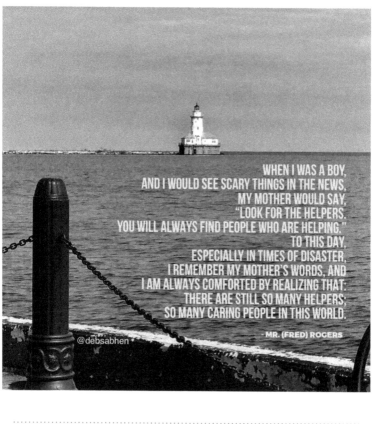

WHEN I WAS A BOY,
AND I WOULD SEE SCARY THINGS IN THE NEWS,
MY MOTHER WOULD SAY,
"LOOK FOR THE HELPERS.
YOU WILL ALWAYS FIND PEOPLE WHO ARE HELPING."
TO THIS DAY,
ESPECIALLY IN TIMES OF DISASTER,
I REMEMBER MY MOTHER'S WORDS, AND
I AM ALWAYS COMFORTED BY REALIZING THAT:
THERE ARE STILL SO MANY HELPERS;
SO MANY CARING PEOPLE IN THIS WORLD.

- MR. (FRED) ROGERS

@debsabhen

There is virtue in work and
there is virtue in rest.
Use both and overlook neither.
- Alan Cohen

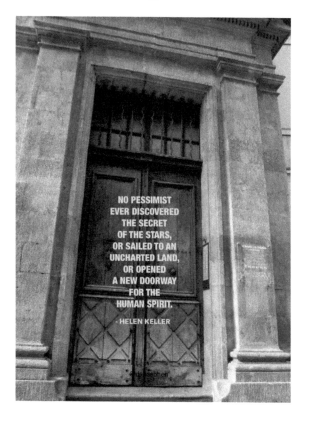

NO PESSIMIST
EVER DISCOVERED
THE SECRET
OF THE STARS,
OR SAILED TO AN
UNCHARTED LAND,
OR OPENED
A NEW DOORWAY
FOR THE
HUMAN SPIRIT.

- HELEN KELLER

Truth is the glue
that holds
government together;
not only our Government,
but civilization itself.
- **Gerald R. Ford**
(from his speech upon taking
the Presidential Oath of Office,
after Nixon's resignation)

LET ALL THE ENDS THOU AIMST AT BE
THY COUNTRY'S THY GODS AND TRUTHS
BE NOBLE AND THE NOBLENESS THAT
LIES IN OTHER MEN SLEEPING BUT
N   SE IN MAJESTY
THINE OWN

EVEN THE SMALLEST ACT OF SERVICE,
THE SIMPLEST ACT OF KINDNESS,
IS A WAY TO HONOR THOSE WE LOST,
A WAY TO RECLAIM THAT SPIRIT OF UNITY
THAT FOLLOWED 9/11.
- BARACK OBAMA

MOST PEOPLE DO NOT LISTEN WITH
THE INTENT TO UNDERSTAND;
THEY LISTEN WITH
THE INTENT
TO REPLY
- STEPHEN R. COVEY

@debsabhen

We have a collective delusion that we need to burn out in order to succeed.
- Arianna Huffington

COULD A GREATER MIRACLE
TAKE PLACE THAN TO
LOOK THROUGH EACH OTHER'S EYES
FOR AN INSTANT?
– HENRY DAVID THOREAU

Ethics and
Equity
and the
Principles
of Justice
do not
change
with the
calendar.
- D. H. Lawrence

There is no comparison
between that which is lost by
not succeeding
and that which is lost by
not trying.
- Francis Bacon

@debsabhon

Sep 17

To know the road ahead,
ask those coming back.
- Chinese Proverb

THE FUTURE
BELONGS TO THOSE
WHO SEE POSSIBILITIES
BEFORE THEY
BECOME OBVIOUS.
-JOHN SCULLEY

As I get older,
I pay less attention to what a man says.
I watch what he does.
– Andrew Carnegie

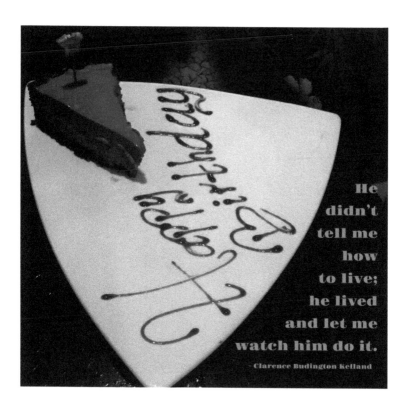

Happy Birthday

He didn't tell me how to live; he lived and let me watch him do it.
-Clarence Budington Kelland

....
....
....
....
....
....

THERE IS A
FOUNTAIN OF YOUTH.
IT IS YOUR MIND,
YOUR TALENTS,
THE CREATIVITY
YOU BRING
TO YOUR LIFE AND
THE PEOPLE YOU LOVE.
WHEN YOU LEARN
TO TAP THIS SOURCE,
YOU WILL TRULY
HAVE DEFEATED AGE.

- SOPHIA LOREN

Gratitude
turns what we
have into enough.
- Melodie Beattie

Educate and inform the whole
mass of the people...
They are the only sure reliance
for the preservation of our liberty.

~ Thomas Jefferson

I don't trust anyone who doesn't laugh.

-Maya Angelou

The eyes are useless when the mind is blind.

- Anonymous

@debsabhen

ALTHOUGH NO ONE CAN GO BACK
AND MAKE A BRAND NEW START,
ANYONE CAN START FROM NOW
AND MAKE A NEW ENDING.

– JAMES R. SHERMAN

IN DEVELOPING TEAMS, I DON'T BELIEVE IN RULES. I BELIEVE IN STANDARDS. RULES DON'T PROMOTE TEAMWORK, STANDARDS DO.
- MIKE KRZYZEWSKI

Sep 29

WHEN YOU COME OUT OF THE STORM,
YOU WON'T BE THE SAME PERSON
THAT WALKED IN.
THAT'S WHAT THE STORM
IS ALL ABOUT.

- HARUKI MURAKAMI

There is real magic
in enthusiasm.
It spells the
difference between
mediocrity and
accomplishment.
- Norman Vincent Peale

@debsabhen

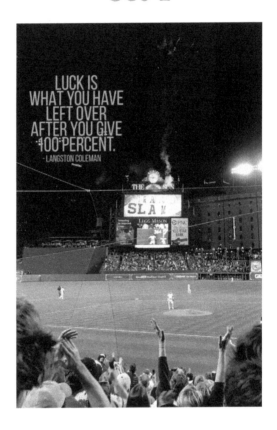

IF MODERATION
IS A FAULT,
THEN INDIFFERENCE
IS A CRIME.
JACK KEROUAC

IT'S REMARKABLE THE LOGIC WE'LL BUILD AROUND MISAPPREHENSION.

— SLOANE CROSLEY

Oct 5

Let us not look back
in anger
nor forward in fear
but around
in awareness.
~ James Thurber

WE MUST BE WILLING TO
LET GO OF THE LIFE
WE'VE PLANNED,
SO AS TO HAVE THE LIFE
THAT IS WAITING FOR US.
—JOSEPH CAMPBELL

@debsabhe

SAFETY RULES
ARE NEEDED TO PROTECT
THE IGNORANT
FROM WHAT THEY DON'T KNOW,
THE IDIOTIC
FROM THEMSELVES, AND
THE INNOCENT
FROM THE ACTIONS OF
THE OTHER TWO.

- AUSTRALIAN
SAFETY POSTER

MEN OCCASIONALLY
STUMBLE
OVER THE TRUTH,
BUT THEY
PICK THEMSELVES UP
AND HURRY OFF
AS IF
NOTHING EVER HAPPENED.
~ WINSTON CHURCHILL

@debsabhen

AFTER A GOOD DINNER,
ONE CAN FORGIVE ANYBODY,
EVEN ONE'S OWN RELATIONS.
- OSCAR WILDE

STYLE IS A REFLECTION OF YOUR
ATTITUDE AND YOUR PERSONALITY.
— SHAWN ACHOR

@debsabhen

Oct 13

As long as we work together—with both urgency and determination—there are no limits to what we can achieve.

— PAUL ALLEN

ONE DOES NOT DISCOVER
NEW LANDS WITHOUT THE COURAGE
TO LOSE SIGHT OF THE SHORE.
— ANDRÉ GIDE

VITALITY
SHOWS IN NOT ONLY
THE ABILITY TO PERSIST
BUT THE ABILITY TO START OVER.
- F. SCOTT FITZGERALD

THERE IS AN INDOMITABLE
QUALITY WITHIN
THE HUMAN SPIRIT
THAT CANNOT BE
DESTROYED;
A FACE DEEP WITHIN
THE HUMAN PERSONALITY
THAT IS IMPREGNABLE
TO ALL ASSAULTS.

- CHESTER HIMES

@deBeabhen

IT IS WISER TO
FIND OUT
THAN
TO SUPPOSE.
- MARK TWAIN

@debsabhen

CONTINUITY GIVES US ROOTS; CHANGE GIVES US BRANCHES, LETTING US STRETCH AND GROW AND REACH NEW HEIGHTS.

- PAULINE KEZER

YOU NEVER KNOW HOW
STRONG
YOU ARE
UNTIL
BEING STRONG
IS YOUR ONLY CHOICE.

- BOB MARLEY

@debsabhen

SOMEONE
IS SITTING IN
THE SHADE TODAY
BECAUSE SOMEONE
PLANTED A TREE
A LONG TIME AGO.
WARREN BUFFETT

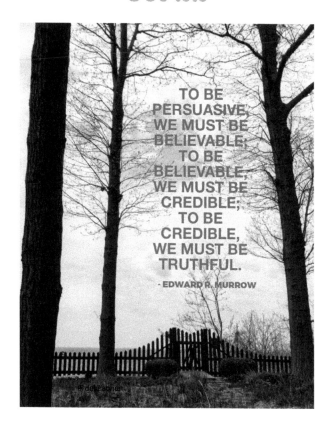

TO BE PERSUASIVE, WE MUST BE BELIEVABLE; TO BE BELIEVABLE, WE MUST BE CREDIBLE; TO BE CREDIBLE, WE MUST BE TRUTHFUL.

- EDWARD R. MURROW

THE SIDELINES
ARE NOT WHERE YOU WANT
TO LIVE YOUR LIFE.
THE WORLD NEEDS YOU
IN THE ARENA.
- TIM COOK

Imagination
is more important
than knowledge.
Knowledge
is limited;
imagination
encircles the world.
—Albert Einstein

Self-care
is giving the world the best of you,
instead of what's left of you.

- Katie Reed

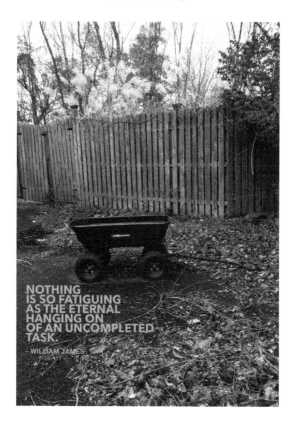

NOTHING
IS SO FATIGUING
AS THE ETERNAL
HANGING ON
OF AN UNCOMPLETED
TASK.

- WILLIAM JAMES

HONESTY IS A VERY
EXPENSIVE GIFT.
DON'T EXPECT IT
FROM CHEAP PEOPLE.

- WARREN BUFFETT

....
....
....
....
....
....

90% OF SUCCESS IS
WAKING UP EACH DAY
WITH A LITTLE HOPE
IN YOUR HEART.
— JASON HALL

SEEING
THE BIG PICTURE
IS NOT AS
IMPORTANT
AS KNOWING
THERE IS ONE.

- MILOS TOMUSILOVIC

A NATION THAT
FORGETS ITS PAST
CAN FUNCTION NO BETTER
THAN AN INDIVIDUAL
WITH AMNESIA.

- DAVID MCCOLLOUGH

They tried to bury us. They didn't know we were seeds

- Dinos Christianopoulos

@debsabhen

We must accept finite disappointment, but never lose infinite hope.

MARTIN LUTHER KING, JR.

TRANSPARENCY
MAY BE THE MOST
DISRUPTIVE AND
FAR-REACHING INNOVATION
TO COME OUT OF SOCIAL MEDIA.

~ PAUL GILLEN

THE MOST COURAGEOUS ACT IS STILL TO THINK FOR YOURSELF. **ALOUD.** - COCO CHANEL

@debsabhen

Change will not come
if we wait for
some other person
or some other time.
We are the ones
we've been waiting for.
We are the change
that we seek.

- Barack Obama

A DEMOCRACY
CANNOT FUNCTION
EFFECTIVELY
WHEN ITS
CONSTITUENT MEMBERS
BELIEVE ITS LAWS
ARE BEING
BOUGHT AND SOLD.
— JUSTICE JOHN PAUL STEVENS

Nov 8

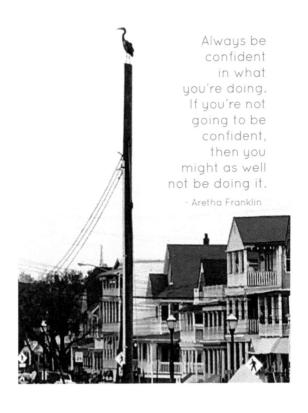

Always be
confident
in what
you're doing.
If you're not
going to be
confident,
then you
might as well
not be doing it.

- Aretha Franklin

AS WE
LET OUR
OWN LIGHT SHINE,
WE UNCONSCIOUSLY
GIVE OTHER PEOPLE
PERMISSION
TO DO THE SAME.
- MARIANNE WILLIAMSON

Peace.
It does not mean to be in a place
where there is no noise,
trouble or hard work.
It means to be in the midst
of those things and
still be calm in your heart.
- Unknown

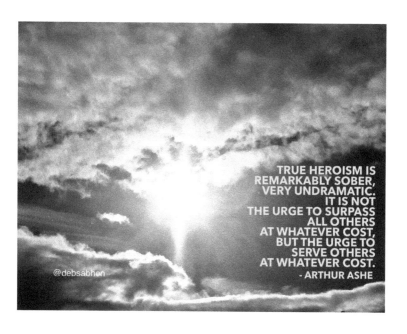

TRUE HEROISM IS
REMARKABLY SOBER,
VERY UNDRAMATIC.
IT IS NOT
THE URGE TO SURPASS
ALL OTHERS
AT WHATEVER COST,
BUT THE URGE TO
SERVE OTHERS
AT WHATEVER COST.
- ARTHUR ASHE

@debsabhen

IF YOU DON'T DESIGN YOUR OWN LIFE PLAN, CHANCES ARE, YOU'LL FALL INTO SOMEONE ELSE'S PLAN. AND GUESS WHAT THEY HAVE PLANNED FOR YOU? NOT MUCH.

– JIM ROHN

THE SECRET OF
CHANGE
IS TO FOCUS
ALL OF YOUR
ENERGY,
NOT ON
FIGHTING THE OLD,
BUT ON
BUILDING THE NEW.
- SOCRATES

@debsabhen

MAN STANDS IN HIS OWN SHADOW
AND WONDERS WHY IT'S DARK.
- ZEN PROVERB

TAKE ACCOUNTABILITY...
BLAME IS THE WATER
IN WHICH MANY DREAMS
AND RELATIONSHIPS
DROWN.
STEVE MARABOLI

@debsabhen

. . . .

. . . .

. . . .

. . . .

. . . .

. . . .

DON'T START YOUR DAY WITH
THE BROKEN PIECES OF YESTERDAY.
EVERY DAY IS A FRESH START.
EACH DAY IS A NEW BEGINNING.
EVERY MORNING WE WAKE UP IS
THE FIRST DAY OF
THE REST OF OUR LIFE.
- BUDDHA

PEOPLE FAIL TO GET ALONG BECAUSE
THEY FEAR EACH OTHER;
THEY FEAR EACH OTHER BECAUSE
THEY DO NOT KNOW EACH OTHER;

THEY DO NOT KNOW EACH OTHER
BECAUSE THEY HAVE NOT
COMMUNICATED WITH EACH OTHER.
- MARTIN LUTHER KING, JR.

You can
edit
a bad page,
but you
can't edit
a blank
page.
– Jodi Picoult

MEANINGFUL ACHIEVEMENT DEPENDS ON LIFTING ONE'S SIGHTS AND PUSHING TOWARD THE HORIZON.

- DANIEL H. PINK

@debsabhen

Better to illuminate
than to merely
shine.

- Thomas Aquinas

Argue for your
limitations,
and
sure enough
they're yours.
- Richard Bach

@debsabhen

. . . .
. . . .
. . . .
. . . .
. . . .
. . . .

If you can,
Help others;
If you cannot,
At least do not harm them.

- Dalai Lama XIV

EXCELLENCE
IS TO DO A
COMMON THING
IN AN
UNCOMMON WAY.
- BOOKER T. WASHINGTON

Nov 24

If you look at what you have in life, you'll always have more. If you look at what you don't have in life, you'll never have enough.

~Oprah Winfrey

@debsabhen

OBSTACLES
ARE THOSE
FRIGHTFUL THINGS
YOU SEE
WHEN YOU
TAKE YOUR EYES OFF
YOUR GOAL.

- HENRY FORD

@debsabhen

GIVING
IS SO OFTEN THOUGHT OF
IN TERMS OF THE THINGS
WE GIVE;
BUT OUR GREATEST
GIVING IS
OF OUR TIME,
AND
KINDNESS,
AND EVEN
COMFORT
FOR
THOSE WHO
NEED IT.
WE
LOOK ON
THESE GIFTS
AS
UNIMPORTANT—
UNTIL WE
NEED THEM.
- JOYCE SEQUICHIE HIFLER

Give light,
and the darkness
will disappear of itself.
—Desiderius Erasmus

Nov 28

AS WE
EXPRESS
OUR
GRATITUDE,
WE MUST
NEVER FORGET
THAT THE HIGHEST
APPRECIATION
IS NOT TO UTTER WORDS,
BUT TO LIVE BY THEM.
- JOHN F. KENNEDY

@debsabhen

Laughter is an instant vacation.
- Milton Berle

Goodbyes are only for those
who love with their eyes.
Because, for those
who love with heart and soul,
there is no separation.
– Rumi

@debsabh...

Dec 1

You have not really lived until you have done something for someone who can never repay you.

John Bunyan

. . . .

. . . .

. . . .

. . . .

. . . .

. . . .

MISSION DEFINES STRATEGY, AND STRATEGY DEFINES STRUCTURE.
-PETER DRUCKER

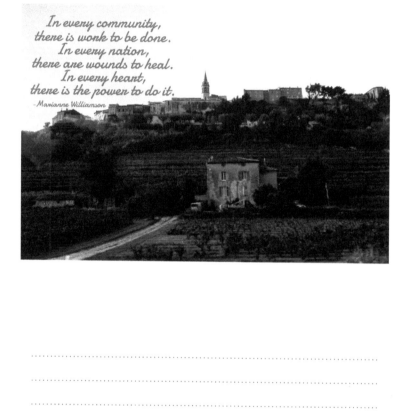

In every community,
there is work to be done.
In every nation,
there are wounds to heal.
In every heart,
there is the power to do it.
-Marianne Williamson

Never ever
mistake her silence
for weakness.
Remember that
sometimes the air stills
before the onset
of a hurricane...

- Nikita Gill

....

....

....

....

....

....

Somewhere,
Something incredible
is waiting to be known.
– Carl Sagan

LEADERS WHO REFUSE TO LISTEN WILL EVENTUALLY BE SURROUNDED BY PEOPLE WITH NOTHING HELPFUL TO SAY.

– ANDY STANLEY

. . . .

. . . .

. . . .

. . . .

. . . .

. . . .

In the dew of little things,
the heart finds
its morning
and is
refreshed.

- Khalil Gibran

Dec 8

Dec 9

IT DOES NOT MATTER
HOW SLOWLY YOU GO,
AS LONG AS
YOU DO NOT STOP.
– CONFUCIUS

I'VE LEARNED THAT YOU CAN TELL A LOT ABOUT A PERSON BY THE WAY THEY HANDLE THESE THREE THINGS: A RAINY DAY, LOST LUGGAGE AND TANGLED CHRISTMAS TREE LIGHTS.

- MAYA ANGELOU

@debsabhen

Dec 11

If you are going to achieve excellence
in big things,
you develop the habit
in little matters.
Excellence is not an exception,
it is a prevailing attitude.

– Colin Powell

Instructions for living a life:
Pay attention.
Be astonished.
Tell about it.
- Mary Oliver

THE
ORNAMENT
OF A HOUSE
IS THE FRIENDS
WHO VISIT IT.
- RALPH WALDO EMERSON

Dec 14

The possible's
slow fuse
is lit by
the imagination.

- Emily Dickinson

UNEXPECTED KINDNESS IS THE MOST POWERFUL, LEAST COSTLY, AND MOST UNDERRATED AGENT OF HUMAN CHANGE.

- BOB KERREY

@debsabhex

LUCK
IS WHAT
HAPPENS WHEN
PREPARATION
MEETS
OPPORTUNITY.
—SENECA

Dec 17

Treasure your relationships, not your possessions.
— Anthony J. D'Angelo

SOME
LEADERS
ARE BORN
WOMEN.
-GERALDINE FERRARO

Dec 19

LISTEN TO THE MUSTN'TS, CHILD,
LISTEN TO THE DON'TS.
LISTEN TO THE SHOULDN'TS,
THE IMPOSSIBLES, THE WONT'S.
LISTEN TO THE NEVER HAVES,
THEN LISTEN CLOSE TO ME--
ANYTHING CAN HAPPEN, CHILD,
ANYTHING CAN BE.

- SHEL SILVERSTEIN

WHAT GOOD IS
THE WARMTH OF SUMMER,
WITHOUT THE COLD OF WINTER
TO GIVE IT SWEETNESS?
- JOHN STEINBECK

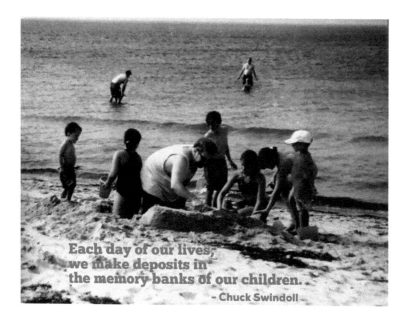

Each day of our lives,
we make deposits in
the memory banks of our children.
— Chuck Swindoll

Dec 22

Looking behind,
I am filled
with Gratitude;
Looking forward,
I am filled with Vision;
Looking upwards,
I am filled with Strength;
Looking within, I discover Peace.
– Quero Apache Prayer

Maybe Christmas, he thought,
doesn't come from a store.
Maybe Christmas, perhaps,
means a little bit more.

–Theodore"Dr Seuss"Geisel,
"How the Grinch
Stole Christmas"

Joy
is the best
makeup.
- Anne Lamott

@debsabhen

The ache for home lives in all of us,
the safe place
where we can go as we are
and not be questioned.

- Maya Angelou

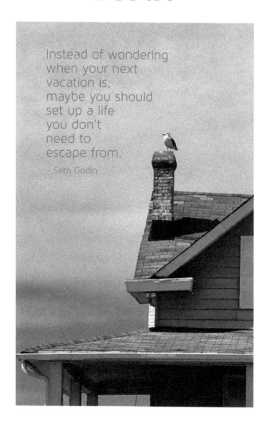

Instead of wondering
when your next
vacation is,
maybe you should
set up a life
you don't
need to
escape from.

– Seth Godin

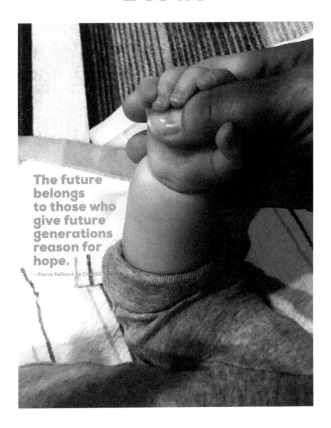

The future
belongs
to those who
give future
generations
reason for
hope.

- Pierre Teilhard de Chardin

Faith goes up the stairs that Love built, and looks out the windows which Hope has opened.
- Charles H. Spurgeon

No distance of place or lapse of time can lessen the friendship of those who are persuaded of each other's worth.

Robert Southey

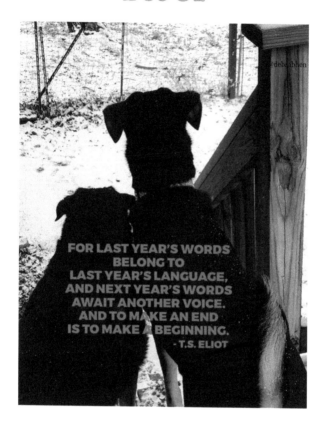

FOR LAST YEAR'S WORDS
BELONG TO
LAST YEAR'S LANGUAGE,
AND NEXT YEAR'S WORDS
AWAIT ANOTHER VOICE.
AND TO MAKE AN END
IS TO MAKE A BEGINNING.
- T.S. ELIOT

A Note from the Author

I hope you have enjoyed this book and that it contributes to your own mindful moments—however you choose to create them. Please feel free to share your ideas and inspirations with me—I would be delighted to hear from you. You can find me on Instagram (debsabhen) and on LinkedIn (www.linkedin.com/in/debsabhen).

I am currently working on another collection of quotations with my photography, and I would welcome your thoughts about what to include and how to organize it. Would you like to see it organized by topic? By the person quoted? Or did you prefer having a "day-book" format with a mix of quotations through each month? If you would like to share your favorite quotations, I would welcome those too!

Wishing you the gift of presence with those you love and those you serve.

With kind regards,

Debbie

About the Author

Debra Sabatini Hennelly lives in New Jersey—close to the ocean and not too far from New York City—with her husband, Bob, an investigative journalist, and their two rescue dogs, Lucy and Leo. Although their three daughters have their own homes now, family time is still a big part of life—which is especially cherished now as new grandparents.

Debbie's passion for finding equilibrium in her own life has been her inspiration for coaching other professionals, helping them lead effectively and develop strategies for resilience. She has more than 25 years of experience creating innovative approaches to fostering ethical leadership and managing risks—from boardrooms to break rooms—in corporate roles and as a consultant.

Debbie is the founder and president of Resiliti (www.resiliti.com), providing consulting and experiential learning for organizations of all sizes. Resiliti focuses on organizational and individual resilience, engaging employees in making ethical decisions, inspiring authenticity and inclusion, and creating risk-aware, speaking-up cultures. She has written articles, delivered keynote speeches and webinars, and created virtual summits on ethical leadership, resilience, unconscious bias, corporate culture, governance, and social responsibility for several professional associations, private clients, and online platforms.

Earlier in her career, Debbie spent more than 10 years in legal and compliance leadership roles in large multinational corporations. Before practicing law, she was a civil and environmental engineer, supervising construction in the oil and gas industry.

Debbie is a proud alumna of Duke University (B.S.E., Civil/Environmental Engineering) and University of Virginia School of Law (J.D.). She enjoys singing, gardening, photography, cooking, genealogy research, exploring the world, and—most of all—spending time with her family.

9 781734 558012